WHY SCIENCE MATTERS

WHY SCIENCE MATTERS

What DOES the Bible say about things scientific?

JOHN NORSWORTHY

Why Science Matters
Published by ConsultEd Publishing
45 Bathurst Crescent, Pyes Pa
Tauranga
New Zealand

ISBN 978-0-473-43167-9 (Softcover)
ISBN 978-0-473-43168-6 (ePUB)
ISBN 978-0-473-43169-3 (Kindle)

Production & Typesetting:
Andrew Killick
Castle Publishing Services
www.castlepublishing.co.nz

Cover design:
Paul Smith

Printed in New Zealand

Now more than ever it's important to know how science and faith interface without undermining each other. In this book John draws on his extensive experience as a teacher to package complex concepts into an easy read. This book is perfect for the average person or student who questions or has an interest in science and God.

Rodney Lake
National Director
Thinking Matters New Zealand

John Norsworthy's love for science and God's Word comes through on every page of *Why Science Matters*. This is a resource that will benefit every Christian educator and anyone struggling to reconcile whether science and the bible are compatible. Refreshingly accessible for the layman and unashamedly biblical, *Why Science Matters* explains why confidence in God's Word was the seedbed for many of the 'fathers' of modern science.

Gavin Clark
Chairman
New Zealand Association for Christian Schools (NZACS)

John Norsworthy's latest book fills a gap in the debate between science and creation. John challenges the notion that science is the enemy of the biblical story of creation. In this easily understood book, John introduces us to some of the world's foremost scientific minds of the past centuries. Here he describes how these great minds were anchored firmly in Christian faith and never doubted that their remarkable research would do anything except enhance our appreciation of God's created world. I'm sure John's book will be valued by a wide audience.

Rev. Craig Vernall
Senior Minister, Bethlehem Baptist Church
National Leader, NZ Baptist Churches

DEDICATION

If you ever thought:

'I don't like science: It's difficult to understand…'

or

'I am uncomfortable with science – it's at odds with my Christian faith…'

or

'I have to study some science, but it's not my thing – I'm more interested in people…'

or

'I think science has nailed the coffin of Christianity…'

Then this book is for you.

CONTENTS

PREFACE

For many years I taught science in high schools and in teacher education, mostly in a Christian context. Sometimes at the beginning of a course I would introduce it with an oral true/false quiz. These are the five statements, believed by many people to be true.

1. Science is neutral. It has no special relationship with any religion or philosophy.
2. Christianity and modern science have always opposed each other.
3. Christianity has nothing to say about science and vice versa.
4. The rise of modern science has brought about the demise of Christianity.
5. You can't be consistently Christian and a good scientist at the same time.

Sometimes I would not tell them my answers but rather suggest that at the end of these lessons they would have clarity about these statements.

My aim is that after reading this small book, you too will have a greater degree of clarity about these statements.

In the same vein as some other things I have written, I raise the question, 'What does the Bible say about this?' Many of us have experienced presentations about how science confirms the authority of scripture. Sometimes, if not often, these presentations 'blind us with science' and we are left wondering, 'What was that all about?' or 'How can I understand that, let alone remember that to tell someone else?' My intention is that this book be quite different. It is not intended to contradict but to complement these ideas. Rather than looking at something of what science has to say about the Bible, this book looks at what the Bible has to say about science and things related to science.

In writing it I have in mind the reader who struggles or struggled with science at school. If this is you, you are in the majority. As I write I remind myself, 'Keep it short. Keep it simple. Keep it faithful to the truth.'

This book is not the result of some ground-breaking research, bringing new light on the topic. I am not an academic or researcher. What I have written has been said by others in various writings and presentations and in a far more erudite and eloquent way in most cases. What I can contribute is a simple clear way of presenting the ideas so that others may catch the concepts and have greater confidence in the Bible as the authoritative Word of God, and will understand where science fits into all of this.

The intention is that this book could be read and discussed by individuals or classes in a church or school setting.

I trust it challenges, informs and edifies you and those with whom you read it.

DEFINING TERMS

What do you mean by that?

1

WHAT IS SCIENCE AND WHAT IS THE BIBLE?

Describing science

The word science comes from the Latin word *scientia*, meaning knowledge and so, in the broadest sense, science is knowledge. However, we use the word science to refer to some systematic way of gaining knowledge and the knowledge thus acquired. As such, science has been part of human life for as long as we have gone about intentionally acquiring knowledge.

In the last few centuries, the European/Western world has embarked on an endeavour to acquire knowledge of the physical or material world through the intentional use of observation and experimentation. This has involved not just recording and organizing the knowledge derived immediately from observation but also the discovery and articulation of general principles or laws that underpin these observable phenomena. I am using the term 'modern science' to differentiate this from the various sciences that there have been since ancient times.

Modern science has been categorized into branches such as physics, chemistry, biology, geology, astronomy, psychology, anthropology, archeology and so forth. These branches are not mutually exclusive. They overlap and mutually inform each other. Often mathematics is regarded as a science as it is used extensively in all sciences and some branches of mathematics, such as calculus, originate from the investigations of scientists.

Observation is fundamental to the methodology of modern science. Typically, scientific method involves observation of phenomena, asking why and how questions about these observations, coming up with intelligent guesses (hypotheses) as answers to these questions, devising further observations through experiments to confirm or deny the hypotheses, and making conclusions. An important part of the method is to record everything done and observed so that others can repeat it and verify its validity and concur with the conclusions or submit alternative conclusions.

Any conclusion, such as a law or principle derived from investigations, must be held with some degree of uncertainty, as there is always the possibility that further observations may disprove the conclusion or reveal the need to reject or modify the principle that has been articulated. It has been said that the only facts in science are the actual repeatable observations.

With this in mind, it is often regarded as doubtful science to make conclusions about things that may have happened in the distant past. They definitely are not scientific facts. Such events cannot be repeated to be observed again. Forensic science, for example, does not establish exactly what happened but merely confirms the testimony of a witness, and we have no human witnesses to our beginnings.[1]

Undergirding the whole modern scientific endeavour are certain assumed beliefs and values. These include:

- the value of knowledge;
- the belief that nature can be understood, the intelligibility of nature;
- the belief that nature runs on orderly principles;
- the belief that these principles are uniform through all of nature, the integrity of the universe;
- the value of discovering simple and elegant principles governing the order of the universe;
- and the value of honesty.

Researchers need to be honest in their reporting and as unbiased as they can in drawing out conclusions.

---

1. Conjecturing about the distant past is interesting and very appealing to some, as it helps give a sense of identity, especially if you don't want to include God in it, but it is not the real core on which modern science is focused. Scientists can observe and seek to understand processes which occur now in the universe, such as the apparent expansion of the universe or natural selection in populations of living things. This is good science. But to then conjecture that these processes, or embellishments of them as in the case of Darwinian evolution, have continued uninterrupted in the past, to explain the origins of the universe or of life and the diversity of living things, is not really science. This is a philosophy of origins posing as science. Such conjectural conclusions cannot be tested scientifically and do not contribute to technological advances and the flourishing of humanity.

Describing the Bible in relation to science

We have often heard it said 'the Bible is not a scientific textbook' and we tacitly agree but are prone to never really think about what that really means. So what is the Bible and what is its relationship to science and in particular 'modern science'?

The Bible is about God and in particular about Jesus Christ, God revealed in human form. Jesus Christ is the focal point of the Bible. The Bible is not set out as a systematic theology, yet it is the source of our understanding of God, our theology. The Bible is God's account of the progressive revealing of Himself to humanity, climaxing in the person of Jesus Christ.

It begins with God revealing Himself as the creator and sustainer of all that is. It highlights the creation of humans who are made uniquely like Him, to relate to Him and to manage Earth with Him. This is found in beginning of the book of Genesis.

It continues to describe the source of the world's problems, our broken relationship with Him, and the nature of the solution to this problem. This progressive revelation involves the use of a group of people, the nation of Israel, to learn this message and host the solution, the Saviour. This is found in the rest of what we call the Old Testament.

It continues to describe the life of the Christ and His work to unlock the solution to the problem (salvation) through His death and resurrection. This is found in what we call the gospels.

It continues to explain this work of Christ, and how to respond to it and work it out in this life, in anticipation of the ultimate restoration of all things to their original purpose and prosperity. This is found in the rest of the New Testament.

The Bible does not propose to teach about the physical structure of the universe and how it works. In comparison to the 'scientific age' in which we live, the original recipients of the message of the Bible had virtually no idea of our cosmology. They had pre-scientific concepts of the world, usually including ideas which are now known to be erroneous, about a flat Earth and about stars moving across the sky and about human physiology. If God were to have taught these people a whole lot of 'scientific' knowledge in the process it would have been a distraction from the real message of the Bible.

The message of the Bible is about *His* relationship to the world, about *His* relationship with us. The Bible is about *His* role in the creation and the sustaining of the world. It is about *His* role in the restoration of humanity and the world and about how we respond to *Him*. It is all about *Him*.

Next we will address the interpretation of Biblical texts which allude to nature, the physical universe and the structure and function of things investigated by modern science.

WHAT DOES THE BIBLE SAY ABOUT NATURE AND KNOWLEDGE?

A science textbook?

2

PRINCIPLES OF INTERPRETATION OF THE BIBLE AND ITS REFERENCES TO NATURE

To correctly interpret any author's writing, including the Bible, we need to follow some basic principles. These include the following:

Background

Consider the *background*. What is the historical, geographical and cultural background? This includes the existing understanding of the topic of the text. This will contribute to us discerning:

- the author's intention,
- the meaning of certain expressions or analogies,
- and how the initial readers would read it.

In particular reference to the topic of this book, we need to consider ideas about the natural world. When the Bible was written, two to four thousand years ago, people had a mix of ideas about the cosmos.

They were something like this: there was a flattish earth with limits to its size. These limits were the ends of the earth. Above the earth was a tent-like structure which held up the sky made of fluid matter (waters) and the stars, sun and moon. These heavenly bodies moved about above the clouds in a set motion from east to west each day and night.

Heaven and earth were considered by most as eternal. They had always been there. Out of the material universe spiritual beings or gods emerged. They were often at odds with each other. The individual natural phenomena associated with and controlled by them ran by their varying whims or rules. A beginning and an originator of everything was usually not even contemplated. The idea of universal rules controlling the cosmos was not possible.

The cosmos is not going in any particular direction. Things go in cycles. Overall, time is not part of a particular progression. Consequently, they did not concern themselves with timelines as we modern westerners do. There seemed to be a pattern in the changes in the sky and on the earth which divided time up into days, months (by the moon), seasons and years (by the sun). It was seen as good to synchronize with these patterns. However, there were other things like storms that did not fit any pattern. They were probably controlled by various powers (gods) within the cosmos. It would be good to appease them too.

In summary, they saw things this way:

- flat earth, earth-centric cosmology,
- the world has always existed,

- the world is going nowhere, it has no purpose,
- gods come out of and are part of the universe,
- gods control their part of the universe (e.g. the sun, the forest, the sea, a certain city of people),
- and, because the world is not progressing anywhere, they were not particularly worried about chronology (timelines etc).

Context

Consider the *context*. By this I mean the text in which it is found. Taking what someone says out of context is a massive error. We need to read at least the chapter in which the text is found, if not the whole book.

What genre (type of writing) is the text?

The ultimate context is the whole Bible. What does the rest of scripture say on the topic? How does this text contribute to the whole?

Meaning

Investigate closer the *meaning* of the words.

When a text is translated from another language there may not be a direct correlating word in your language.

The words may be an idiom or other form of speech peculiar to the author's time and place. Consider the literal (plain) meaning first before extracting allegorical or poetic meaning which may also be there.

Application

Ask the question, 'so what?' This is a matter of application. How does this inform us? How does God want us to respond? What could I, the reader today, do in response to this?

The next chapters look at a brief sample of texts which speak of, or allude to, the natural world, the focus of science. They have been chosen to illustrate these principles of interpretation and to draw out the main tenet of scripture on the topic.

3

REFERENCES TO NATURE IN THE BIBLE: THE GENESIS CREATION STORY

Genesis 1 is the initial and hence the most significant reference to the cosmos in scripture. Therefore, it demands a chapter of its own.[2]

Background

The writer, Moses and the initial recipients, the people of Israel lived in a world uninformed by either the Bible or modern science. To understand this passage, we need to step into their world and their thinking. Resist the temptation to interpret it in the light of subsequent Christian and scientific thinking, until you have first got the intended meaning.

The cosmology and concept of gods and ideas about time spoken of earlier are particularly relevant. If God is going to

---

2. If you have scanned this book to find out what the author has to say about the days of creation, and plan to read this section to pass judgment on the whole book, you do us both an injustice. Please read this in the context of the whole book!

reveal truth to these people about Himself in relation to the world, He is not going to confuse the message by arguing about their cosmology. That is why the text has 'unscientific' terminology that sounds like their ancient ideas about the shape of the cosmos.

The genre

The book of Genesis is historical narrative. This means it is the story of events reported by those who witnessed them. Research such as archaeology confirms it is accurate history. The very beginning of the book, the story of creation is an introduction to this history and by nature does not fit neatly into the genre of reported history. It is still totally reliable truth but not strictly 'historical' truth. It is 'pre-historical' truth.

Clearly the story is told in a patterned form. The repetition in the pattern is there to emphasize the truth being conveyed. We should give attention to the repeated expressions to see the main meaning.

The main message

At the risk of oversimplifying it, or of reading too much into text, here is what I see are the main points of what God is saying in it.

In the beginning…

Immediately the readers were confronted by a new idea. The

world had a beginning. It has not always been there as they had assumed.

God created the heavens and the earth…

God, *Elohim,* is a plural word used as a singular word. It has the sense of the most holy 'other'.

God exists and is a fellowship, the ultimate diversity in unity.

God is not part of the universe but pre-exists it. He is eternal. He created space and time and all that is in them. This confronts and contrasts dramatically with the ideas of deities these people would have held.

All that exists did not just happen. This answers the question, 'Why is there something, rather than nothing?'

It was purposefully made! It has meaning! It is not a product of chance processes. It is not just a cosmic accident!

The earth was without form and void…

The word 'was' has the sense of 'becoming' and so could be rendered, 'in the process of becoming it was'. If it was shapeless, 'the earth' may well mean, at this stage, 'the matter that makes up the earth', a legitimate use of the word 'earth'.

Highlighting formlessness and emptiness is a hint that what is to come is describing two things, the shaping and the filling of the world.

There are various ideas on how this works out in the text. Some commentators suggest that days one, two and three are describing three aspects of forming and days four, five and six are describing three aspects of filling. Rather than one chronological sequence of six days, some suggest these are two sets of sequences.

The framework view suggests six ideas about creation expressing a logical rather than a chronological order:

Forming:		***Filling:***	
Day 1	Light energy (and hence the form of matter)	**Day 4**	Lights in the sky
Day 2	Fluid matter: sky and sea	**Day 5**	Creatures filling the sky and sea
Day 3	Dry land masses and vegetation	**Day 6**	Land creatures: animals and humans

And darkness was over the face of the deep...

There was nothing to see yet. There was the absence of light. There was no input of what we call energy yet. This was to come from the 'Spirit of God' moving. Until this comes nothing can change and hence time is meaningless.

Then God said...

This is the first repeated phrase. It is the introduction to each day. It is the chief clue to the point of each day. We need to delve deeper.

Words were considered more than mere emissions of sound. They were powerful extensions of one's being, communicating information and ideas.

This concept of God's words, or Word is subsequently developed through the Bible. For example, Psalm 19 which is referred to in the next chapter. The second section of verses (9-11) uses five words to describe God's word or speech; law, statutes, precepts, commands and the fear of the Lord.

This gives the idea that when it says 'God said', He was putting into place laws or principles which shaped and governed what He created, and that these laws need to be respected and obeyed. The initial recipients would have sensed something of this.

This expression, 'then God said' is repeated eight times in the story, the beginning of each day and twice on days three and six. It suggests eight times of *information input* into creation, of *special creating power* as distinct from sustaining power.

The New Testament writers, especially when writing to people of non-Jewish background and thus less familiar with the teaching of the Old Testament, express the concept of God, and hence Christ, being the creating and sustaining Word. For example, see John 1:1-18 and Colossians 1:15-17.

Let there be light...

Light, piercing the darkness and formlessness, needs to be the first aspect of creation.

Have you ever thought of the idea that when God said, 'Let there be Light,' He was putting into place the principles that hold the universe together, that determine the relationship between matter and energy, the laws that scientists are discovering and expressing in terms such as $e=mc^2$ and $f=ma$. This would enable the atoms to form, and thus the shaping of the universe. Of course, the original hearers most likely would not have thought this, but maybe we with the hindsight of modern science can!

God called...

In a similar way to 'God said', the expression 'God called' has implications of more than just a name. It implies some power or purpose. It reflects the idea of organizing and classifying His creation. Day and night, the arrangement of the sun and stars and the seasons have specific purposes. They have a reason, God's reason.

The evening and the morning were the...day...

Why 'evening and morning' rather than 'morning and evening'? The word 'evening' has the sense of 'making obscure', the onset of darkness, the lack of revelation. The word 'morning' has the sense of unfolding, dawning or revealing. Thus this expression conveyed a sense of bringing into the light, moving from nothing to something, of lifelessness to being fully alive, a wonderful expression of each phase or aspect of God's creation.[3]

Subsequently, Jewish tradition has the night as the first half of the full cycle of a day.

The first day, the second day…the sequence of days…

Remember, the first hearers would not at first be looking for a timeline of creation. Other things would have stood out to them.

God did not create it all at once. God had a plan, a strategy. It was an organized process. He created the necessary environmental structures before creating the creatures to go in them.

This was not a random spontaneous series of acts. This was in stark contrast to the spontaneous acts of the capricious gods the first hearers were prone to believe in. Typical so called 'creation stories' of the time were really stories of the conflicts of various gods and princes. Creation myths from around the world typically involve the conflict of beings such as gods or princes and the subsequent fanciful (from our scientific point of view) creation of some part of the world. Thus the acts of

3. In talking about reality, the ancient Greek philosophers used the terms 'cosmos' to speak of the world and world order and 'chaos' to speak of the absence of it. Thus we could say this expression indicates God bringing reality from chaos to cosmos.

'creation' were unintended by-products of the interaction of spiritual beings.

This orderly planned sequential speaking into existence of creation defies these types of stories.

And God saw that it was good...

From our perspective, when we research the intricacies and enormity of His creation we would say it is overwhelmingly awesome. But God, who is greater than all of His creation, said it was good. This was saying that the various parts of creation had value. This value was in themselves. They may have been useful to us, but their value was not because of their use, but because God saw that they were good.

God saw everything He had made and indeed it was very good...

This was after He created humans. It implied that humans were of highest value to God. It suggests that the whole of creation working together in the harmony of its designed order is extremely valuable.

Let Us make man in Our Image...

Prior to this God said, 'let there be', but in making man He said, 'let *Us* make man in *Our* image'. The plurality of His being, as expressed in the name *Elohim*, is highlighted. The ultimate unity in diversity was to be reflected in humanity.

The 'image and likeness' of God has multiple layers of meaning. Amongst these are the characteristics of God He has already revealed in the previous verses of the story, such as:

- God is fellowship, so humans are to live in fellowship,
- God speaks His Word so humans are able to communicate information and ideas,
- God is intelligent so we are able to 'think God's thoughts after Him',
- God is a creator-worker so we are created to creatively work like Him,
- God is the law-giver and so we are created to rule over or manage the earth with Him,

And God blessed them...

Woven through the story is the clear indication that God is not an impersonal influence. He has purpose. He declares things into existence. He blessed His creatures. He extended the grace of life and the ability to reproduce to them.

God said ... fill the earth and subdue it ... have dominion over ... living things.

God had a purpose for humanity. It was to manage the earth. This included the development of the resources of the earth. Of interest to this topic, it was this impulse in humanity which led to the necessary scientific investigation which would come later.

God had a planned relationship of humans to living things. It was not to exploit and destroy but to manage the living world.[4]

> *And on the seventh day God ended His work … and He rested…*

God ceased from His creating. This suggests that there is a distinction between His supernatural information adding and creative activity, which was the subject of His work in the six days, and His ongoing sustaining activity that continues throughout and into the day of rest.

It is the sustaining work, rather than the supernatural creative work, which is the subject of scientific investigation. It is this which can be repeatedly observed and tested. We can observe and describe the products of His creation but not His actual process of initial creation.[5]

---

4. It is currently popular to accuse the Bible of inspiring the exploitation of the environment, quoting this verse. The issue is not taking dominion of the living things, but how that is done. Do we 'do our own thing' or first listen to the voice of God in creation? In our time, modern environmental scientists have embraced this charge to manage the welfare of living things, not to exploit and destroy but, as good stewards, to be responsible for their flourishing. Many don't appreciate that this moral obligation, this burden of responsibility, comes from God's Word.

5. Some suggest that miracles are God breaking His sustaining rules, implying that He, in doing so, is unfaithful. But on the other hand they could be seen as God invoking (speaking into operation) His higher rules, His creative word.

In summary

More could be said about Genesis 1 and 2, but enough has been highlighted to convey the main message.

Genesis 1 is all about *God* and *His* acts of creation. It is about *the creator*, not the details of His creation. It is not about the physical process but about *the processor, God Himself*. It is about how *He* did it, about *His* creative *word*, not about how it physically happened, or shaped up. It is about *why* things are, *His* purposes, not the details of *what* is. It is about *His* purpose and *His* highly valuing and blessing *His* creation. It is consequently about *His love* for His creation and, in particular, for us created in His image.

Discussion

Imagine you are a person living in ancient Egypt or Canaan. You can't read but someone tells you the story of Genesis 1. What about it strikes you as strange or disturbing because it threatens your view of the world?

4

REFERENCES TO NATURE IN THE BIBLE: OTHER PASSAGES

1 Kings 4:29-34

This passage describes the wisdom of Solomon. This included some of what we call scientific knowledge. 'God gave Solomon wisdom and very great insight ... He described plant life, from the cedar tree of Lebanon even to the hyssop that grows out of walls. He also taught about animals and birds, reptiles and fish.' The implication is that he listened to God by studying and describing living things. In line with the instruction of God given to Adam, who observed and named the animals, Solomon was a biologist, and a taxonomist.[6]

Proverbs 6:6-8

This is part of Solomon's wisdom. 'Go to the ant, you sluggard. Consider her ways and be wise.' God can give us scientific

---

6. A scientist who classifies and names living things.

knowledge through our observation so that it can help us understand practical wisdom.

Proverbs 8

In this chapter 'wisdom' declares to be there during creation. For example, 'When he prepared the heavens, I was there' (v27). God's wisdom was an integral part of the deliberate process of creating all that is. It is of note that in the Septuagint, the ancient Greek translation of the Old Testament, the word 'wisdom' is translated 'logos', and in English 'the Word', the word the gospel writer John uses to refer to Christ, the creator and sustainer of the world.

Ecclesiastes 1

In Ecclesiastes, the preacher Solomon addresses the philosophical problem of the futility or meaninglessness of life when lived without reference to God. In Chapter 1 he speaks of life going round and round – one generation passes and another comes – the sun rises and sets and goes back to rise again – the wind goes round and round. Clearly this passage is not teaching about the movements of the sun but rather the apparent purposelessness of life.

The preacher goes on to say that he devoted himself to study and to explore to gain knowledge about everything under the sun, but it only brought the grief of meaninglessness. Solomon learned that science will not answer the basic philosophical questions of life – of meaning, purpose, value and ultimate reality.

Job

In this book God addresses the issue of suffering, and the endeavour to find the specific reason for a person's suffering. The book of Job is most likely the oldest of the books of the Bible. As such it was written before anything of the Old Testament revelation was written. The only 'written' word of God was His creation. At various places in the book, references are made to a whole range of geological, astronomical, meteorological, anatomical and biological phenomena. The purpose of this is not to describe details of nature but to point out the mighty sustaining power of God over His creation.

For example, in Chapter 26 Job speaks of the wisdom and power of God over nature:

> *He spreads out the northern skies over empty space:*
> *He suspends the earth over nothing.*
> *He wraps up the waters in His clouds.*
> *Yet the clouds do not burst under their weight.*
> *He covers the face of the full moon,*
> *spreading His clouds over it.*
> *He marks out the horizon on the face of the waters*
> *for a boundary between light and darkness.*
> *(Job 26:7-10)*

In the middle of responding to his critics, Job says,

> *'ask (or inquire of) the animals and they will teach (or point out to) you, or the birds of the air, and they will tell (or show) you, or speak to (or meditate on) the earth, and it will teach you, or let the fish of the sea inform you. Which of these does not (make you) know (or ascertain by observation) that the hand of the Lord has done this? In his hand is the life of every creature and the breath of all mankind.' (Job 12:7-11)*[7]

In other words, do science to learn about God.

At the end, in Chapters 38-41, God at last has His say. He addresses the presumption that we should know the reason for everything. He quite abruptly confronts Job with the question about who He is and who Job is in relation to the whole world. He says such things as, 'Were you there when I laid the foundations of the earth?' and 'Have you commanded the morning since your days began and caused the dawn to know its place?' This tirade goes on for four chapters.

Many references to nature are quite 'unscientific' in their expression. He is relating to Job and the readers in the language of *their* understanding of the world, not the language of modern science.

God is making important points. We do well to recognise these truths, such as:

---

7. Explanation of words added.

- He made it all and we are mere creatures.
- It is His wisdom and His command that sustains it all.
- He knows it all and we know almost nothing.[8]
- He is totally awesomely 'out of this world'. There is nothing in the whole universe comparable to Him.
- An examination of the things of nature, scientific observation clearly shows that it is God who sustains it all.
- If we listen to Him we might learn something of His knowledge.

Psalm 19

This psalm talks of the two main ways God reveals Himself – through His creation and through His written Word and of our response of humility, conviction and meditating on Him.

The psalmist once again uses terms that fit the idea of the sun living in a tent-like framework in which it moves from one end to the other. This is not according to our scientific understanding of the cosmos but it connects with the initial hearers who did not need to be distracted from the message of the psalm. This is of no matter as the psalm is not teaching cosmology, the shape of the universe but rather teleology, the purpose of the universe.

The purpose of the heavens is to declare the glory of God.

8. I find it ironic, if not sad, that there are modern atheistic philosophers who suggest that science has just about revealed the answers to almost everything!

In verses 2 and 3 it says the heavens utter speech revealing knowledge to the whole world. This is a blatant invitation to us to listen. God invites the human race to conduct astronomy and learn about *Him*.

Psalm 29

In this psalm the psalmist speaks of various aspects of thunder storms. For each aspect he begins, 'The voice of the Lord'. Storms are not random acts of nature or of the gods of nature. God is speaking in the storms. The usual first idea we have is that He is speaking judgment but if one reads the whole psalm it is clear He is speaking about His power, His majesty and His glory. The psalmist invites the readers to listen to the voice of God in nature. In response, 'The Lord gives strength to His people. The Lord blesses His people with peace' (v11).

As we will see later, this is the invitation to which the early modern scientists responded.

Psalm 97:1-6

In a similar way to Psalm 19, this psalm declares that natural phenomena are subject to God and that they demonstrate that He reigns and declare His righteousness.

Isaiah 40

This text mentions 'the circle of the earth'. Some have said, 'See, the Bible teaches that the earth is spherical'.

If we read the whole chapter we find that Isaiah is talking about the greatness of the Lord in relation to His creation. Amongst other things he says humanity is like grass. We are here one day and gone the next but God's word endures forever.[9]

He is like a shepherd and we are like the sheep. He knows the measurements of the whole earth. He doesn't need us to inform Him. It is He who sits above the whole (circle) of the earth and we are like grasshoppers. It is He who stretches out the heavens like a curtain and like a tent for things to dwell in.

If I talk about my 'circle of friends' I do not mean they stand around me in a 360 degree circle. I am referring to all the people to whom I relate as friends. If he is teaching that the earth is circular, he is also teaching in the same verse that the heavens are held up in a structure like a curtain. Isaiah is using the concept, commonly held by the people of the time, that the stars are held in place by a structure like a canopy over the earth. He is not teaching that this is actually so. He is teaching that God is the great creator and sustainer of the universe and that if we meditate (wait upon) Him we will renew our strength like the eagles. We will 'run and not be weary, walk and not faint'.

As we will see later, the message of Isaiah 40, repeated in various ways throughout the Bible, is fundamental to the discipline of science and that these ideas are foundational to the rise of modern science.

---

9. This reference to His Word is interesting when you consider the ideas about the relationship between His Word and creation discussed in the commentary on Genesis 1.

Jeremiah 33:19-26

Jeremiah is speaking of God's faithfulness to His promises to Israel and David. To emphasise the certainty of His promise, God says that if His covenant with day and night does not stand and if He had not ordained the fixed patterns of heaven and earth, then He would also reject Israel. It is clear that the prophets like Jeremiah were certain that God held together the whole order of nature by His dictates, His laws of nature.

Revelation 7:1

'I saw four angels standing at the four corners of the earth, holding the four winds of the earth.' If we were to interpret this literally, in the concrete sense, we would say that the Bible teaches that the earth is a square and the winds are somehow generated in each corner. Of course we do not do this. We know that the book of Revelation is an apocalyptic book using picture language and symbols to convey its message. The ancients thought of the earth as they would a building which normally was rectangular with four corners. The four corners of the earth are a bit like the four compass points, north, south, east and west. We know that the text is not referring to a physical reality.

Isaiah 11:12, Matthew 24:31, Mark 13:27

In a similar way, each of these verses speak of God gathering people from the four quarters, winds or corners of the earth. Clearly the Bible is not teaching that the earth has four corners. These are examples of the idiom meaning everywhere in the Earth.

Matthew 6:26-34

In teaching about worry, Jesus said, 'Consider the birds of the air… consider the lilies…' as illustrations of God's providence. God's faithful sustaining power seen in nature should be of encouragement to us to trust Him.

Colossians 1:15-17

This explains that the expression 'He is the firstborn of all creation' means that He is the creator of all things. He is also the purpose of their creation. Then in verse 17 Paul adds, 'and in Him all things hold together.' God in Christ is the active sustainer as well as the creator of all things.

In summary

- This is just a sample of Biblical texts related to the natural world. Do we get the message?
- The world is God's idea. He is the creator and sustainer of all that is.
- He created and sustains the world by His Word, that is His command, His intelligence, His power.
- He made us to be in on the management of the earth in relationship with Him. We need to understand what we are managing.

- He speaks in creation and invites us to listen, and be blessed in fulfilling His purpose for us.
- We do well to listen and obey!

We are going on to see in history what happened when people not only believed this but actually did this, but before that let's have a look at what the Bible says concerning knowledge.

Discussion

Imagine you are King Solomon. The Queen of Sheba has just arrived and asks you questions about things in the natural world. How would you shape your description of them? What big picture message would you want to convey?

5

A BIBLICAL UNDERSTANDING OF KNOWLEDGE

The philosophical study of knowledge, how we know what we know, is called epistemology. To get a handle on where science fits into this, we as Christians must have some understanding of what the Bible says about knowledge.

What does the Bible say about the nature of truth and knowledge – our understanding of truth? What is there to know and how do we know what we know?

The Bible is full of words about truth and knowledge. This chapter just outlines some key principles.

The apostle John has a particular contribution to this. Any reader of the Bible will be struck by the words of Jesus recorded in John:

'...you will know the truth, and the truth will set you free.' (John 8:32)

'I am the way, the truth, and the life. No one comes to the Father, except through me. If you really know me you will

know the Father as well. From now on, you do know him and have seen him.' (John 14:6,7)

'Now this is eternal life: that they know you, the only true God, and Jesus Christ, whom you have sent.' (John 17:3)

'the reason I was born and came into the world is to testify to the truth. Everyone on the side of the truth listens to me.' (John 18:37)

If we learn nothing else from John about knowledge, we learn that the ultimate knowledge is the knowledge of God. This is particularly gained through knowing God the Word, Jesus Christ and that gaining this true knowledge brings freedom.

What ultimately is there to know?

The Bible teaches that an understanding of God and who He is in relation to who we are, i.e. the fear of the Lord, is the basis of knowledge and wisdom (Proverbs 9:10).

Knowledge ultimately is comprehension of the self-revelation of God and to know Him constitutes the purpose of eternal life.

As referred to in the previous chapter, Psalm 19 outlines some important principles about knowing God. It is worth studying.

The first section of verses begins with: 'The heavens declare the glory of God…' and continues to say how the parts of the heavens (the universe as we now call it) speak forth God's revelation, His knowledge.

The next section of verses begins with: 'The law of the Lord is perfect ...' and continues to say how the Word of the Lord (in particular the Bible as we now call it) is so adequate and effective.

The final section of verses begin with: 'But who can discern their own errors?' and speaks of the humble introspection that results from listening to God's revelation.

How does God reveal Himself?

Through Creation: The universe is the revelation of God. From the cosmos to the subatomic, from the function of a pine tree to the quirks of human thought and behaviour, the created order reveals the nature and character of God. Humans, who are created 'in God's image', are especially reflections of God, even though distorted by sin. Creation is often called God's general revelation. It is available to everyone to 'read'.

> *...what may be known about God is plain to them, because God has made it plain to them. For since the creation of the world God's invisible qualities – his eternal power and divine nature – have been clearly seen, being understood from what has been made, so that people are without excuse. (Romans 1:19,20)*

Through His Word: The Bible is a record of God's progressive revelation of Himself, climaxing in the person of Jesus Christ, who is the ultimate revelation of God in person, 'the Word made flesh'. The Bible is God revealed in words for us to get to know Him and is applicable to all of life (2 Peter 1:9-21).

Where does science fit into this?

Science is the interpreting of nature to reveal God's truth about His creation. Science is listening intently to the voice of God in creation. The diagram below summarises these ideas:

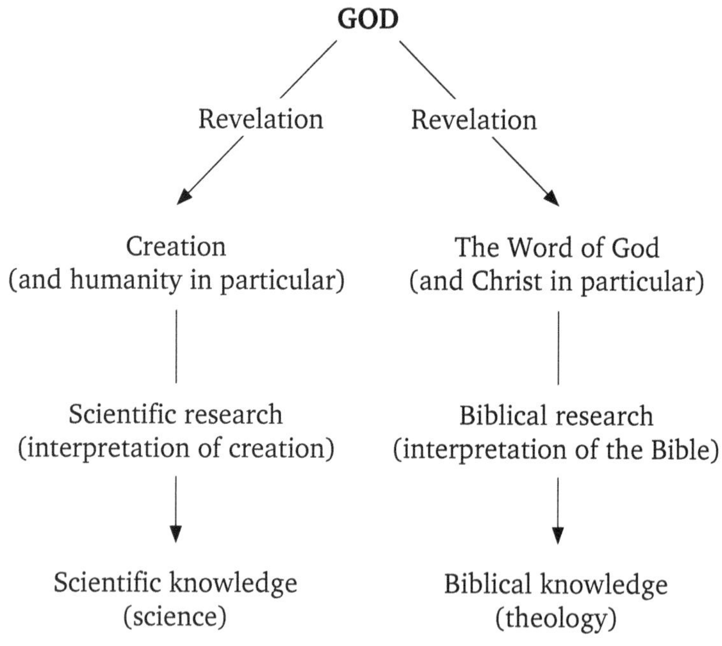

How we obtain knowledge

Now that we have considered what truth there is to know, let's think about what faculties God has given us to obtain knowledge.

We are drawn to the writings of the apostle John again, this time his first epistle, in which he speaks often about knowing the truth and about the love of God in us.

The first thing he does is appeal to the readers on the basis of real observation.

> *That which was from the beginning, which we have heard, which we have seen with our eyes, which we have looked at and our hands have touched – this we proclaim to you concerning the Word of life. The life appeared; we have seen it and testify to it. (1 John 1:1,2)*

A fundamental way of acquiring knowledge is *observation*, the use of our senses. Our senses are very limited, but God has given them to us to observe His creation, including human social phenomena. Without them we can neither discover new knowledge or take in what others have discovered. As John was demonstrating in his introduction, it is by means of our senses that we come to faith. Paul said, 'Faith comes through hearing the message, and the message is heard through the word about Christ.' (Romans 10:17)

John next goes on to speak about being honest with ourselves. Otherwise we lie and do not live out the truth, and we deceive ourselves and the truth is not in us. *Honesty*, particularly about ourselves, is an integral part of true knowing. Intellectual dishonesty or irrationality is a sure way to miss knowing the truth. The Bible has stories of people reasoning together to come to a knowledge of the truth. The truth is reasonable and logical. God gave us our minds to deduce the truth. *Reason* is a means to gaining knowledge.

Some ancient Greeks considered reason to be the only way to truly know. To deny knowledge by observation is not only obviously wrong, it is also not Biblical. The Bible itself is based on observation of real historical phenomena, not just ideas. As will be explained elsewhere in this book, it was this Biblical understanding of the use of observation in conjunction with reason which contributed to the rise of modern science and technology.

Then John goes on to speak about obeying the truth. 'The man who says, 'I know him', but does not do what he commands is a liar, and the truth is not in him. ... Whoever claims to live in him must walk as Jesus did.' (1 John 2:3-6) The Greeks saw knowledge of the cognitive nature as an end in itself. They would say that I have learned when I know. The Hebrews saw knowledge in a far more practical way. Cognition was not an end in itself. Jesus commissioned His disciples to teach all that He had taught them to *do*. Hebrews would say I have learned the truth when I *do it*. John speaks of that 'doing' as loving God and loving others. James also speaks of this when he says, 'be doers of the word, not hearers only, deceiving yourselves…' (James 1:21-27).

John also alludes to the witness of the Spirit. '…this is how we know that he lives in us: We know it by the Spirit he gave us' (1 John 3:24). God is still in the business of 'inspiring us by the Holy Spirit'. The Greek word *oida* used in scriptures such as Romans 8:28 ('We know that in all things...') has this idea of intuitively knowing. The scripture also uses expressions such as 'by faith we know...' (e.g. Hebrews 11:3). This may be considered *a priori* knowledge – knowledge based on agreed presuppositions.[10]

How do we know what we know?

- *By observation:* the use of our senses.
- *By reason:* the use of the mind.
- *By faith:* the use of our intuition.

Pulling it together

What must be appreciated regarding ways of knowing is that we cannot safely use one of them in isolation.

Intuitive knowledge claiming to be the voice of the Spirit which defies reason or observation is not knowledge at all but dangerous deception. It could be called epistemological mysticism.

Rational knowledge without the witness of observation can well prove to be false, as did Aristotelian cosmology. This is pure idealism or extreme rationalism.

---

10. One may ask about 'common sense'. I contend that 'common sense' is inherently unreliable in that it is shaped by a commonly held world view and culture. Before Galileo, Aristotelian cosmology was considered common sense. Contemporary western society now hosts divergent world views and so we are discovering that what we called common sense is now no longer common.

Belief that only that which is observable by the senses is real is called scientism or empiricism.

Way of knowing	By use of	Error when made the ultimate way to know
Observation	Bodily senses	Empiricism, scientism or positivism
Reason	Mind	Rationalism
Faith	Spiritual intuition	Mysticism

Rationalism, empiricism and mysticism are all inadequate approaches when used in isolation for the acquisition of knowledge. Rather, 'in the mouth of two or three witnesses' knowledge is established. The Biblical way of knowing involves all three working not separately but together.

Similarly, God's general revelation and special revelation are not to be approached in a dichotomous way, that is, with a sacred/secular segregation of knowledge. It was the Biblical understanding of God as orderly and principled which kick-started the modern scientific revolution. It was Newton's theological quest, occupying most of his time, which led him to scientific research. See the next chapters for more on this.

Scientific and Biblical research should assist each other. With this in mind, some Christian learning institutions talk of being informed by research and faith.

Since creation and the Bible are both God speaking they, by definition, will not disagree. If it appears that science and the Bible are in conflict, we can deduct that it is a case of bad science and/or bad Biblical interpretation. From my experience, I suggest it is often both. We see in the creation/evolution debate elements of both.

Applied knowledge

Finally, to truly know we must put into practice what we know. Believing the truth is relying on it by trusting it and living in the light of it. True faith or knowledge is doing it! Modern technology is just this – modern science applied to the real world. The knowledge acquired by scientific research has been believed and applied.

Scripture repeatedly speaks of the blessings of knowing, believing, trusting and obeying the truth it reveals. For example, Deuteronomy 28 is a whole chapter describing the blessings of obeying God's law, the law of Moses and the curse of not knowing or ignoring it and not putting it into practice. In parallel to this is the blessing of discovering, believing and putting into practice God's laws of science. The blessings of life with modern technologies that we take for granted are the result of knowing and obeying God's laws of nature. This will be discussed in Chapter 7.

Discussion

What is your reaction to or understanding of each of these statements about science?

- Science is the study of the creation.
- Science is acquiring detail to our understanding of God's general revelation.
- Science is a God-ordained activity.
- Science is a way of knowing but not the only way of knowing as empiricists think.
- Science involves observation, reason and intuition but specifically involves observation.
- Science is learning how God sustains the universe.
- Science is listening intently to the voice of God in creation.

Can you think of something where it is believed that science and the Bible disagree? Can you discern where there is wrong interpretation (of creation and/or the Bible)?

THE RISE AND FALL OF MODERN SCIENCE

Where did that come from?

6

THE FOUNDATIONS OF MODERN SCIENCE

In our time modern science is a phenomenon which pervades the whole world, but it was not always so. Have you ever wondered why modern science and the technology that arose from it happened in Europe and the Western world and not elsewhere in the world? Have you ever asked why it has only arisen in the last 500 or so years and not 2300 or 1700 years ago?

What was it about Europe about 500 years ago that was the catalyst for modern science to occur? As Christians we could glibly say, 'It must be because it was Christian'; but so was Rome (officially) in the year 400, and France in 800.

It was something about the way people were thinking in the time prior to the modern era.

Science in a general sense was part of all ancient civilizations. For example, there have been technologies arising out of careful testing (trial and error), such as various weaving industries around the world. Basic machinery was developed. There was careful observation and reasoning, such as we see in the brilliant Chinese records of the stars' movements, but no attempt to delve into the reasons for these movements in a 'modern scientific' way. They did not look for universal principles which governed nature and movements of the stars. They observed and recorded the recurring nature of these movements and then attempted to fit their lives into these patterns. This idea occurred in most ancient and more recent civilizations. We call it astrology, as distinct from the branch of modern (and ancient) science, astronomy.[11]

Their concept of the order of nature was not that there were constant principles, but that there were cyclical powers at work, or that nature was controlled by capricious spirits. Their careful observations were not for the purpose of getting understanding of the physical principles but rather to be in harmony with the rhythm of nature or to please the god of that part of nature.

In various ways, the thinking of their cultures actually prevented the rise of what we now call science.

In contrast to most of the world, the thinking of the founders of modern science was shaped by a culture that was predominantly Christian. Sometimes they were rebelling against the establishment, which was religious. However, it was not against their Christian faith and culture. They were in fact advocates, defenders, and promoters of their Christian

---

11. Astrology is not all bad as some Christians are inclined to think. For example, the magi who brought gifts to the child Jesus were ancient astrologers who used their precise knowledge of the appearance of comets and alignment of planets with the constellations of stars as signs of significant events. This is just one of several examples of astrology in the Bible.

faith. They often asserted that their discoveries confirmed their faith.

Biblical Christian theology (or world view) was the key factor in shaping modern science.

In the later middle ages the first universities developed. They were an extension of the ministry of the church to teach the emerging church leaders philosophy and theology as the unifying foundation of all knowledge. Academics began to explore the outworking of Christian thought into all areas of life. For example, the writings of Jean Buridan, who was the rector of the University of Paris in the 1300s show that he considered the implications of God being the creator and sustainer of everything that is. The rules that govern the bodies in the heavens must be the same as those governing things on the earth. So, as he thought about the emerging idea of the earth being a rotating sphere, he considered projectile motion and celestial motion and the rotation of the earth in this light. This Biblical view of God's principles applied universally was a direct rejection of the prevailing ideas from Aristotle.

Sir Francis Bacon, the 16th and 17th century philosopher and father of scientific thought, considered the contrast between a Biblical view of God and that of pantheism, the idea that god or gods are part of the universe. Things made demonstrate the power and skill of the workman, not his image. Similarly, the works of God show the omnipotence and wisdom of God, not His image. In this regard heathen pantheism differs from the sacred truth. They suppose the world to be the image of God, and humans to be an extract or image of the world.

This pantheistic view has resulted in the hindrance of further discovery.

These *Biblical concepts of God and humanity* were at the heart of the work of the first modern scientists:

1. God is *the only God who created everything*. If there are various creator gods there will be various rules by which these creations run. There will not be a consistent principle to find.

2. God is *the original creator. He created everything out of nothing*. Only He is eternal. Matter and the universe are not eternal. Therefore, they have a reason to exist. The universe is not a meaningless accident! With this undergirding our thinking, our curiosity is directed to discover the ultimate reason.

3. God is *distinct from His creation.* He is the original cause. Cause and effect are not confused. So we can look for cause and effect. Pantheistic views of reality caused this distinction to be confused.

4. God is *personal and so has a will*. Thus He can choose for the universe to run according to His will, according *to His laws of nature*.

5. He is *all powerful* and can enforce His laws on everything He wills to obey.

6. He is *faithful* and chooses to apply His will consistently.

7. God is *rational*. Therefore, His creation is ultimately going to be *intelligible*. Therefore, we can pursue an understanding of it.

8. Humans were created in the *image of God*. He is a thinking God and He has made us to be thinking creatures. Johann Kepler is reported to have said, 'think God's thought after Him'. Hence to discover the principles of God through science is a privilege of the human race.

Added to this were their ideas about *knowledge*:

1. Knowledge of the truth was not a human construct but rather a reception of revelation. Truth was seen as not just within the human mind, but as something outside the mind to be sought after using the mind. Reason alone was not the channel of all truth. This was in contrast to the Greek (Aristotelian) philosophy, idealism, which was prominent in the late middle ages.[12]

2. All knowledge of truth was a result of God revealing Himself, whether it be through the book of scripture,

---

12. In our age, postmodern thinking has reverted to the idea that truth is a construct of the mind.

the Bible or the book of nature, God's creation. Nature was not a playground for various gods and spirits to do unpredictable things. It was not an illusion, nor was it inherently evil, as pagan beliefs would have it. Nature was God speaking, God revealing Himself.

3. History was not just a cycle of birth, death and rebirth, as conceived by many ancient and eastern belief systems. Time was linear not cyclical. History was going somewhere. Progress could be made. History was the unwrapping of God's revelation. There was still something new to learn. Without this belief, why seek it?

4. Observation was a valid source of knowledge. As early as the 13th century this idea was being promoted. It found reception in the minds of Christians open to a Biblical epistemology:

- Robert Grosseteste (1175-1253), Bishop of Lincoln, insisted on the need for observation and experimentation in the study of nature, and mentored Roger Bacon.
- Roger Bacon (c1212-1292), a Franciscan monk with an Augustinian philosophy slated those who put more trust in the ideas of philosophers than in observation. He saw the value of testing an hypothesis. He is often regarded as a major forerunner of modern science.
- William Ockham (c1280-1349), lecturer at Oxford,

wanted to purify Christian theology from the contamination of pagan Greek metaphysics (view of reality). His attack involved forming an epistemology where knowledge about the world is based on experience of individual things.

5. The Reformation re-alerted them to the principle that knowledge of the truth was gained from the written Word of God rather than church tradition or the ecclesiastical priesthood. This gave them spiritual license (but not always legal license) to not conform to traditional church dogma, but to think 'outside the box' and be guided by the promptings of the Bible.

6. Truth was not personal and private. Interpretation of reality was open to the scrutiny and judgment of others in the light of the Bible. The Bible gave a basis for public consensus and evaluation of claimed truth.

7. God's revelation was to be interpreted simply.

   The church fathers saw four ways to interpret scripture – firstly (and foundationally), literally, then allegorically, morally and eschatologically. The church of the Middle Ages was caught up in interpreting scripture symbolically or allegorically as the primary way to understand what it was saying. This hermeneutical (interpretive) strategy for reading the book of God's word, the Bible, also shaped the reading of nature.

> However, the Reformation restored the literal sense of the interpretation of scripture to its primary place and with it came a literal approach to reading creation. Galileo Galilei, for example, did not argue about the fundamental philosophy of the church but rather was urging a literal reading of nature – the true language of nature.

Added to this was their *concern for righteousness, Christian ethics*.

Honesty was an integral part of their moral compass. They set the example for the scientists who were to follow in their footsteps.

Truth and truthfulness are basics of science. Science is committed to finding the truth which is not just a personal belief but an objective truth.

Science is dependent upon the cooperation of scientists to be as honest as possible in their reporting of their discoveries. There is no place for corruption. When it occurs it leads scientists down dead-end lines of investigation. When it is exposed it discredits the whole scientific community. Therefore, scientists have to explain their research in such a way that others can repeat their experimentation and check that it is true.

With this understanding of the foundations of modern science, we could say that the Bible is the mother of modern science.

Discussion

Imagine you were a 16th century atheist who believes everything is here by random processes. If there is no all-powerful lawmaker, why would you look for universal laws governing the world? How would you respond to these monks and clerics suggesting we could discover something of God by observing nature?

7

THE FOUNDERS OF MODERN SCIENCE

Building on these Biblical ideas God-fearing people began to investigate His creation in a disciplined manner. They became the 'fathers' of many of the fields of science we recognise today. Here is an overview of 20 such people.[13]

Johann Kepler (1571-1630)

Kepler was the founder of physical astronomy. He was popular for his astrological charts and calendars. However, he believed in God the lawgiver and so deducted that He governs the world by orderly principles. He conceived that a God who spoke the world into existence by simple words would not create it to run on a discordant number of epicycles, but rather something simpler and more powerful. Since we are created

13. Various writers have compiled lists like this. My list is a brief selection. For many of them I have drawn on information from the book, *Men of Science, Men of God* by Henry M Morris PhD, in which he lists over 100 scientists. (See reading list at end of book)

in His image we have the capacity to think something of how God thinks and so understand these powerful orderly laws by which He governs the universe.

Kepler wrote, 'Since we astronomers are priests of the highest God in regard to the book of nature, it befits us to be thoughtful, not of the glory of our minds, but rather, above all else, of the glory of God.'

Kepler's faith has been rewarded with the discovery of the simple laws of nature. Over the following centuries and through many struggles against prejudices to the contrary, scientists found that quite simple laws of nature do actually apply. This is still the expectation of scientists. It arose from Kepler's belief in the Bible.

These days there are scientists who have adopted Kepler's faith in science without believing in the foundation of that faith.

Blaise Pascal (1623-1662)

Pascal was a great mathematician. His work laid the foundations for hydrostatics, hydrodynamics, differential calculus and the theory of probability. We may recognise his name in the unit of pressure, Pascal. He is known for his faith in God and is credited to have first expressed what is now called the Wager of Pascal, which goes something like this: 'How can anyone lose who chooses to be a Christian? If when he dies there turns out to be no God and his faith was in vain, he has lost nothing. He has been happier in life than his non-believing friends. If, however, there is a God, heaven and hell, then he has gained all while his unbelieving friends will have lost everything.'[14]

Robert Boyle (1627-1691)

Boyle is one of the fathers of modern chemistry. He lived in England and Ireland in the generation that had the Bible in English (the King James version) and so studied and delved into its truth. He was adamant that God gave us His world to observe for ourselves rather than just believe what ancient philosophers had said. In academic circles this was an unpopular stance. As a result of his careful observations he uncovered basic principles about gases such as air. He shared his discoveries in public demonstrations of experiments. He was a key person in establishing the Royal Society for Improving Natural Knowledge. He said that from a knowledge of God's work we shall know Him. As an active believer he financially supported Christian missions and Bible translations.

William Petty (1623-1687)

Petty was involved in the founding of the discipline of statistics. His work laid foundations for the modern study of economics. He wrote many articles sharing evidence of God's design in nature.

---

14. It is interesting that recent mathematicians have used probability theory to show that the chances of everything existing as it is, by chance processes alone, is one in a number too huge to imagine – probably more than the number of atoms in the universe!

John Ray (1627-1705)

Ray was considered the greatest zoologist and botanist of his time. He wrote a book called *The wisdom of God manifest in the works of creation*.

Nicolas Steno (1631-1686)

Steno was the father of stratigraphy. He worked on the premise that rock strata and the fossils in them were laid down rapidly by catastrophic events such as the flood of Noah.

Sir Isaac Newton (1642-1727)

Newton is considered the greatest mathematician of his time. In his pursuit to describe the motion of the planets around the sun, he invented what we now call calculus. He discovered and described mathematically the law of gravity. He established statements of the basic laws of motion. He investigated light and developed the particle theory of light propagation. He invented the reflecting telescope.

Newton was firstly a believer in God and wrote many books on the Christian faith. When I attended university our physics lecturer said, 'Newton spent only about 10% of his working life on mathematics and physics. What could he have achieved if he had not spent the rest of it on theology?' If I had known what I know today I would have felt like calling out in the lecture, 'Nothing. He would have lost his motivation!' Newton was about demonstrating the existence and wisdom of God in nature. Like many others of these early scientists he used his science as Christian apologetics (defence of the faith).

Carolus Linnaeus (1707-1778)

Linnaeus knew that God created various living things to reproduce according to their kind. He expressed that he attempted to systematically define these original kinds. His system of classification is still the basis of modern scientific naming of living things. Thus he is known as the father of biological taxonomy.

John Dalton (1766-1844)

Dalton was the father of atomic theory. He was involved with the Society of Friends (often referred to as Quakers) and Christian education and was a firm Bible-believing Christian.

Georges Cuvier (1769-1832)

Cuvier is considered to be the founder of comparative anatomy. He was involved in the study of fossils and was one of the movers to establish the science of palaeontology. As a staunch creationist he participated in some of the early debates with pre-Darwinian evolutionists.

Michael Faraday (1791-1867)

The Faraday family belonged to a group of non-conformist Christians called Sandemanians. Faraday had a love for the Bible and lived his life guided by the Bible and prayer. He was involved in the leadership of his church.

In his youth he came to read the newly-published writings of current pioneers of chemistry. He came to work for one of them, Sir Humphrey Davies. He developed a love of science, reading God's book of works alongside the Bible, God's book of words. He made contributions to the field of chemistry, but his main scientific achievements were in the field of electricity. He discovered the relationship between electricity, magnetism and motion and thus invented the electrical generator. He is considered one of the greatest physicists of his time.

Charles Babbage (1792-1871)

As a firm believer, Babbage amongst other things wrote a defence of the Bible and miracles. He developed information storage and retrieval systems and used punched cards for sets of data and instructions in automated industrial controls. Thus he is considered the father of computer science.

Matthew Maury (1806-1873)

Maury noted that Psalm 8 spoke of 'paths in the seas' and so chose to investigate and chart winds and currents of the Atlantic Ocean. Hence, he is known as the father of oceanography.

Louis Agassiz (1807-1873)

Agassiz was a great palaeontologist and the father of glacial geology. As he believed God specially created every kind of organism, he spoke out strongly against the ideas Darwin was promoting.

James Simpson (1811-1879)

Simpson discovered chloroform and laid the foundation for anaesthesiology. He said his biggest discovery was finding Jesus Christ as saviour. He said he became fascinated with the idea of Adam's sleep as God made Eve out of his side. This motivated him to his research.

Gregory Mendel (1822-1884)

As a monastic monk, Mendel was responsible for the monastery garden. He prayerfully and mathematically studied the breeding of peas with various characteristics and thus discovered the foundational ideas of genetics. He rejected the idea of extending these principles about variations of living things to Darwin's general theory of evolution.

James Joule (1818-1889)

Motivated by his Christian faith, Joule discovered the mechanical equivalent of heat, the foundation of thermodynamics. The unit of energy, the Joule is named after him.

Lois Pasteur (1822-1895)

Pasteur was the father of bacteriology. Convinced that only God can create something out of nothing, he was determined to prove that germs arose only from existing germs. He persistently argued against the idea of spontaneous generation of living things and clashed with the promoters of the rising popular Darwinian ideas.

William Thomson, Lord Kelvin (1824-1907)

Lord Kelvin formally established the statements of the first two laws of thermodynamics. As a Christian with conviction, he saw that Darwinism and the ideas associated with it defied these basic principles and so opposed them strongly.

James Maxwell (1831-1879)

Maxwell is the father of electromagnetic field theory. Einstein spoke of his work in these terms: '...The most profound and most fruitful that physics has experienced since the time of Newton.' Acknowledging Christ as his saviour, Maxwell said that God's original command to man to subdue the earth provided the personal motivation to pursue his scientific work.

For the purposes of this book I have curtailed my list to these notable 20 who conducted their work before the 20th century. I could have added many more including Edward Jenner, Joseph Priestley, Thomas Anderson, Joseph Gilbert, George

Washington Carver, Joseph Lister, William Ramsay, John Fleming and Werner Von Braun, all of whom were leaders or founders in their field.

Although less well-known, there were a number of women involved in early modern science. For example, Emilie du Chatelet (1706-1749) was a French philosopher who focused on Newtonian natural philosophy. She wrote extensively on the foundations of physics and knowledge. Included in her work are an analysis of Genesis and the Bible, and arguments for the existence and nature of God.

Of course there were also scientists who, for various reasons, did not overtly express their faith in Christ or a commitment to Biblical truth, and others who did not believe but worked within the values of modern science.

Some of the early scientists mentioned above may have entertained some unorthodox doctrine. For example, some struggled with the doctrine of the trinity. However, this does not detract from the fact that these men were inspired by the revelation of the Bible and were guided by its values and ethics. It was Biblical truth that moved and guided them, that gave birth to their science.

Many of these 'fathers' of modern science, such as Boyle, Newton, Faraday, Dalton and George Washington Carver, saw no separation of their spiritual and scientific quest. They were motivated to discover God as He spoke in creation. They sought the Lord as they enquired. Newton said that all of his discoveries were wrought by prayer. Is this where he got his great hypotheses? Thus to study the sciences (physical and human) and their application in various technologies is a 'spiritual' activity. Prayerful use of observation and reason is thoroughly Biblical.

There are numerous biographies of these men, some written for children and young people to read.[15] They are inspiring stories.

In conclusion, it is clear that modern science was an outworking of a Biblical understanding of the world and humanity.

Discussion

If you were a science teacher in a Christian school, how would this chapter cause you to shape your lessons? How would you integrate history, Biblical studies and science?

15. For example, see the list at the end of the book.

8

THE FRUIT OF MODERN SCIENCE

Applied in technology

During the Middle Ages, monks lived out the belief that God made us to work to manage the earth and serve others. They developed various technologies to alleviate the drudgery of work. The water wheel and horse collars are just two examples. Added to this, modern science has enabled the development of the vast range of technological advances that we have experienced in the last few centuries:

- Astronomy and cosmology led to the ability to navigate around the world with precision. This opened up efficiencies in global transport and trade.

- Medical science has led to the virtual elimination of dreaded infectious diseases which plagued humanity. As a result, the life expectancy of the citizens of developed countries is something in the order of three times what it used to be.

- Electrical science has led to the development of a vast number of devices that make life more pleasant and tasks more efficient than ever imagined in times gone by.

- Biological science has enabled us to manage food production and animal welfare in much better ways than in the past.

- Computer technology has revolutionized our ability to store and communicate information.

The list could go on! The flourishing of societies who have embraced the developments stemming out of science is unparalleled in all of history.

Obeying the 'word' of God

People have listened to the voice of God in creation, even if they have not recognized it as His voice. They have embraced the conclusions of this investigation as the truth about reality. Thus they have trusted these laws of nature, which we as believers in the Biblical revelation see as God's laws. Then, driven by their desire to develop the earth, they have used these laws to develop powerful means of making life more fulfilling. The result is an extraordinary difference in human flourishing.

In the book of Exodus, we read how God, through the leadership of Moses, called the nation of Israel out of Egypt. He then established the foundations of the nation, the 'Law of Moses'. The bulk of Exodus, Leviticus, Numbers and Deuteronomy spell out the details of this set of laws to govern the nation. They covered various aspects of community life, including social relations, public health regulations and ceremonial celebrations. All were seen as laws expressing their relationship to Him.

The law is prefaced by promises of flourishing, like, 'If you listen carefully to the Lord your God and do what is right in His eyes, if you pay attention to His commandments and keep all His decrees, I will not bring on you any of the diseases I brought on the Egyptians, for I am the Lord who heals you.' (Exodus 15:26) Then, at the end, Deuteronomy 28 lists the blessings of obedience and cursings (negative consequences) of disregarding and disobeying them. Clearly listening to God's laws, believing them and putting them into practice would bring about a huge difference of flourishing as a community.

Just as listening to and obeying God's special revelation brings blessing, so too does listening to and applying God's general revelation bring blessing.

The Bible is the key

The Bible is the key to human flourishing. When technological application of science is motivated by the principles found in both the Old and the New Testaments, the gospel of Christ and the love of God, humans have been blessed.

The diagram introduced in Chapter 5 appears on the opposite page in a more complete form. Note the arrow indicating the link between the knowledge of the Bible and the modern scientific endeavour, and the arrow indicating the need for the application of technology to be guided by the principles of the Bible.

However, history has worked out less simply than this! All is not good in our world. Science and technology will not eliminate sin from the human heart. When motivated by alternative agendas, modern technology has been the tool for adding to human misery. For example, it has been used to create tools of crime and war, as well as the exploitation of the poor and vulnerable. Especially in cultures uninformed by the values of the Bible, we have struggled to bring the benefits from technology to all.

Modern technological advances have contributed to environmental degradation. Some have blamed science for this but rather it is because not enough science, or not enough application of ecological science has occurred. We have not listened intently enough to the voice of God in nature or failed to obey.

Finally, there is the denial of the foundations of science, which the next chapter goes on to describe.

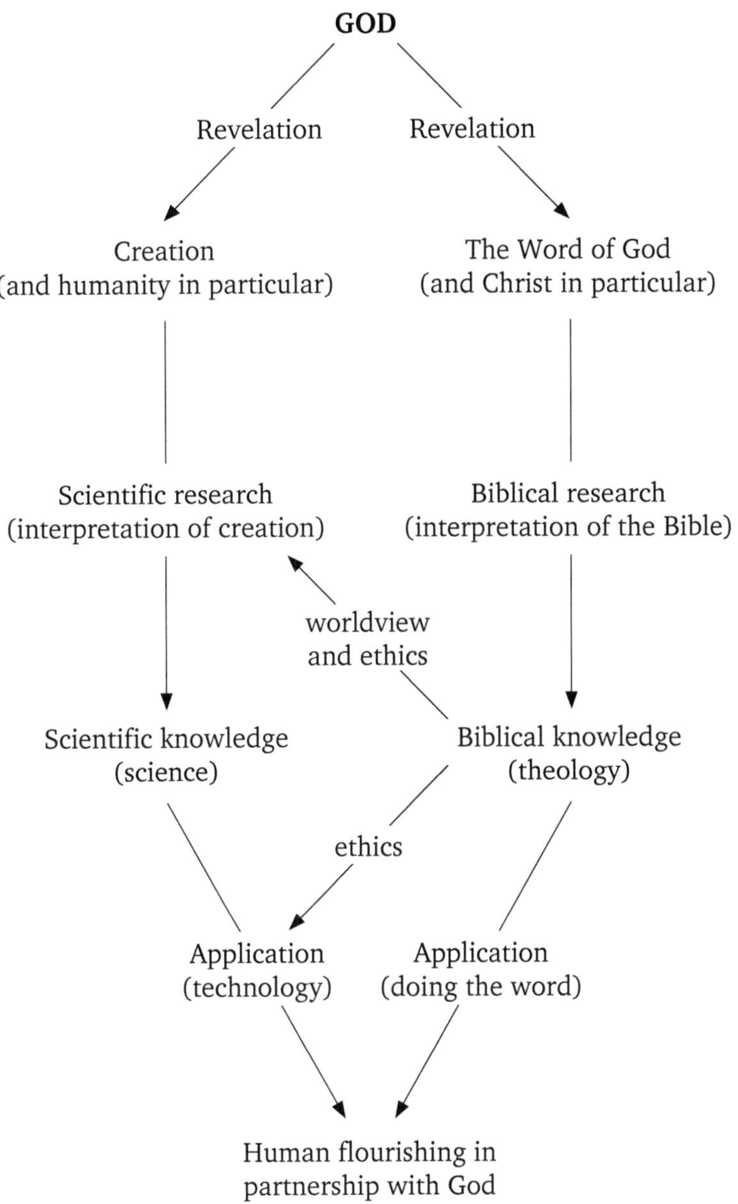
GOD
Revelation
Revelation
Creation
(and humanity in particular)
The Word of God
(and Christ in particular)
Scientific research
(interpretation of creation)
Biblical research
(interpretation of the Bible)
worldview
and ethics
Scientific knowledge
(science)
Biblical knowledge
(theology)
ethics
Application
(technology)
Application
(doing the word)
Human flourishing in
partnership with God

9

LOSING THE FOUNDATIONS, LOSING THE PLOT

In identifying the world's need for salvation the apostle Paul describes a downward spiral of affairs that occurs in a society where humans 'suppress the truth in unrighteousness'. The first step is denying the message of the natural world.

> *What may be known about God is plain to them, because God has made it plain to them. For since the creation of the world God's invisible qualities – His eternal power and divine nature – have been clearly seen, being understood from what has been made, so that people are without excuse. For although they knew God, they neither glorified him as God nor gave thanks to Him, but their thinking became futile and their foolish hearts were darkened. Although they claimed to be wise, they became fools. (Romans 1:19-22)*

He then goes on to describe the collapse of civil society.

This process of degeneration of society is repeated every time the denial of God's revelation or the neglect of passing it on to the next generation occurs. The time of the rise of modern science is no exception. Running parallel to the exciting revelation of God's laws of nature came a rejection of God.

Deism

People who were set on avoiding God began to have an inflated idea of the achievements of science. They began to believe that they had demonstrated that the universe is sustained by natural processes alone and that God is not involved. They overlooked the observation that all physical objects seem to be compelled to obey laws of nature. Instead they imagined that living things including humans, and indeed the whole universe, were mere machines, rather than seeing God as actively involved in sustaining His creation.

However, they could not work out how to explain origins without God. This general belief that God created and then retired to let it all function by itself and for us to work out life by ourselves without His help is usually called deism. Many key figures of the Enlightenment were deists. Some like Benjamin Franklin were men of science too.

Darwinism and Materialism

Following on from this was the rise of the concept of evolution by natural processes alone. The general idea of a process not involving God being responsible for our origins was not new but at this time it gained momentum. Darwin and his followers proposed a way to eliminate God from creation. Many of them did so tentatively because they wished to remain in the establishment that purported to believe in God and that was firmly entangled with the established church. Others made it their firm belief – their world view. For example, Thomas Huxley, sometimes called 'Darwin's bulldog', was a great promoter of science as the only way to know and put his evolutionary world view at the centre of his projects including developing teacher education. So for them science became deified as the ultimate or only way to know, hence the term 'scientism'.

This way of viewing the world is variously called scientism, materialism or secular naturalism. It generally has these basic ideas (presuppositions):

1. About knowledge: The only way to truly know is through observation or research.

2. About reality: Everything is essentially physical. Even the most complex living things including humans, are just physical machines or organisms made up of chemicals.

3. About meaning: All of nature is purposeless, the product of chance processes. Hence, all apparent progress is ultimately open-ended random change.

4. About matter time and eternity: Matter is eternal. The laws of nature are fixed. They always were and always will be.[16]

The strength and control of these ideas on those who hold them is not because they have arrived at them through critical thought. Rather, they captivate the mind of most because they are uncritically assumed.

It is this world view, scientism, not real science, that opposes the Bible.

This book is not the place to describe the 'unscientific' nature of the general theory of evolution. It is quite clear to discerning observers that, at its core, this theory is a philosophy of origins, a cornerstone of secular naturalism, a belief system stemming from a denial of the creator and sustainer of the universe. It operates under the guise of being science. It assumes that the rules by which the universe runs now (which we see as the sustaining word of God) are the only principles that have ever existed, and rules out, without any evidence, the possibility of a creator.[17]

Sadly for some, the mindless processes of evolution became the rationale or the justification for their moral decisions. Injustice could be justified as natural selection. If natural selection was the way we have come to be, then some con-

---

16. The idea of the universe having a beginning as proposed by both the Bible and the 'big bang' theory do not sit comfortably with believers in 'scientism'.

17. Added to this, the scientific evidence for the theory does not stack up but this is not the topic of this book.

sidered black people to be less evolved and factory workers to be 'less fit' and so able to be exploited by the more fit. Eugenics became promoted by others. Prompted by philosophers such as Friedrich Nietzsche, the idea of evolving into a superhuman race was embraced by others. Its logical but extreme manifestation involving the elimination of the 'less fit' was subsequently played out by Nazism.

Modernism or Positivism

Building on this 'scientism' was the rise of 'modernism' or 'positivism', the belief that through science and education we will be able to answer all of life's challenges and usher in a new age of prosperity and fulfilment. Saint-Simon, Compte, and Bertrand Russell were some of the spokesmen for this school of thought. This move was epitomised by the blind and arrogant faith in science and technology displayed by the owners of the Titanic. This positivism could not stave off a period of world war, economic depression and more world war.

Postmodernism

These heralded a move of disillusion in science and the modernist utopianism, which began to take hold in the 1960s. This 'postmodernism' has cast off this optimism and embraced a belief that logically stems out of naturalism, that everything is a result of random, mindless processes. There is no universal truth to discover, and the only truth is that which you personally make of things. You construct your own truth. You make sense of things in your own way.

This postmodern approach to truth has disturbed many conservative scientists and mathematicians, both Christian and otherwise. Belief in truth behind natural phenomena, independent of human recognition of it, is a fundamental pillar of modern science. Is this move away from seeing truth as objective going to jeopardise the future of science? Will a philosophy that sees science as the way we make sense of the world and which can vary from person to person and from time to time, be able to sustain the objective nature of scientific knowledge? Is post-Christian and post-modern philosophy the beginning of the end for science?

It is of interest that there are some evolutionary philosopher/scientists who recognize that there is scientific evidence that we may be more than mere machines. In an attempt to avoid the idea of an intelligent creator, they suggest that even the 'laws' of nature and physical constants, like the gravitational constant (G) and the speed of light (c), have evolved and so are no more than changing 'habits' of nature. Linked to the idea of an evolving cosmic soul, or 'panpsyche', this philosophy posing as science is similar to pantheism. Is this a completion of the circle, back to pre-Biblical Christian thinking about nature?

Aggressive atheism

Thus, we find influential philosophers and scientists (or would-be scientists) promoting a world view which undermines science itself. We find them lambasting the Christian faith, saying science has brought us enormous advances including the elimination of diseases and suffering, while Christianity has brought us nothing but prejudice and fear. I am reminded of the apostle's words, 'suppressing the truth in unrighteousness' (Romans 1:18).

They reject the historical reality that the Bible is the mother of modern science. This rejection of the Bible is much like someone observing an older woman in their life who thinks she can tell them what is right and wrong. Not recognising that she is their mother, they decide that she is not responsible for their existence, is redundant (and even dangerous), and should be eliminated!

All is not lost

Despite a common perception in the western world, the Christian faith is growing fast numerically. Today, globally, there are more people reading the Bible or being influenced by the ideas and values of the Bible than ever before. This means that, given sufficient numbers of people embracing the Bible, the spiritual and material 'blessings' that come with the influence of the Bible will spread to other parts of the world.

Discussion

Richard Dawkins has written something along these lines: 'I am against religion because it teaches us to be satisfied with not understanding the world.' Is there an element of truth in this statement? What does he mean by 'religion'? What really is the truth on this matter?

Discuss the five statements in the preface of this book. What clarity do you now have about these statements?

CONCLUSION: WHAT ARE WE DOING?

So what?

10

HOW TO RESPOND

This brief chapter is a compilation of some thoughts that summarise and complement what has been said in this book.

> *God is not simply an alternative explanation for the same things that science explains. He is the one who created the universe that science explains. Science is the practice of studying the secondary causes of things, the mechanism by which God makes them happen. Science is no magic wand. It is an enterprise that has been very successful, for all its flaws, at understanding the way in which the universe works. It does not, however, and cannot give ultimate explanations for why things are the way they are. We can go further than that. It is only because the universe was created by God that science is possible at all. We are able to study and understand the universe because God created it. Science does not dismiss the need for God. On the contrary science is possible only because of God. (Kirsten Birkett)*[18]

18. christianschools.org.au/attachments/article/164/birkett.pdf

In this book I have attempted to make clear that the Bible is not a scientific text book but it is the mother of science. The Bible does not attempt to teach any details about how nature works but it explains the One who makes it work. It does not spell out the secondary causes but declares the primary cause.

Creation and the Bible have a common message

As explained in Chapter 5, both the Bible and Creation are God's revelation of Himself, and hence they will not contradict each other. If you think the Bible and science disagree on something, it is a problem of interpretation – bad interpretation of creation, bad science and/or bad interpretation of scripture.

Amongst the common messages of the Bible and science are these:

The Bible	**Creation**
The Bible says that God created by His information-containing and powerful Word.	Creation demands a creator. From the smallest subatomic particle to the most complex living thing creation is loaded with intelligent design.
The Bible says that God sustains by His Word.	Creation and in particular life requires a sustainer. Random processes won't hold it together.
The Bible says that God is glorious, almighty, all-knowing, faithful etc.	Creation displays various aspects of His person and character – His glory etc. He faithfully applies His laws to all of creation.

The Bible urges obedience to its revelation – with obedience comes the 'blessings' of human flourishing and with disobedience 'cursings' of suffering.	Creation demands obedience to the rules – with obedience comes blessings and with disobedience evil and suffering.

The common message is about God.

What the Bible says about the nature of creation

In the beginning God made it. It is finite. It was not eternally there. It is finite in both time and space.

God has ordained that it is structured and operates in orderly patterns. This order is described as His upholding Word. This order is waiting to be observed, discovered and described. The science of mathematics is all about this order. Without this belief there was no reason to discover this order. This belief motivated modern science. Since it is God-ordained, we need to respect and conform to this order to fulfil God's purposes.

It is constantly changing. Creation may operate according to consistent principles of an eternal God but creation itself is perpetually subject to change. It is reasonable to assume the principles are constant but foolish to assume the particulars of creation are the same as they were in the past or will be in the future. (Psalm 102:25-27, Isaiah 40:6-8, 51:6, Matthew 6:19, Hebrews 1:10-12)

It was created perfect but has been spoiled by sin. Not just the human race, but the whole of creation has been adversely affected by our sin. This is related to God's judgment upon sin. This is the possible main cause of likely differences between creation particulars in the past and the present. (Genesis 3:17-19, Isaiah 24:4-7, Romans 8:20-22)

What the Bible says about our understanding of creation

It is very limited. God knows it all; we hardly know anything at all. Christians should never entertain ideas of grandeur about our mastery of scientific knowledge. (Job 26:7-14, Job 38-42, Psalm 8:3-4, Ecclesiates 3:11)

Our research and resultant understanding is impaired by our sin. Scientists may claim to be objective but always bring into their scientific procedure and thinking certain biases. In particular, we leave God out of our view of the creation. (Romans 1:18-32)

Scientific discovery will not guide us into truth and right living. The special revelation of the Bible is needed for this. Science cannot be used to determine the answers to basic presuppositions – the ontological (what is real), teleological (what is the purpose) epistemological (knowing) and axiological right and wrong and value). Science will neither tell us where we come from nor lead us to Utopia. (Psalm 19, Psalm 119 e.g. v9, Ecclesiastes 1:12-18, 1 Corinthians 2)

What the Bible says about the method of scientific discovery and acquisition of scientific knowledge

Divine insight, inspiration. 'God gave Solomon wisdom and insight.' (1 Kings 4:29) The best hypotheses are God-inspired. Hence, the best scientists are men of prayer.

Direct observation and research. God invites us to observe. This is distinct from just seeking the opinion of those who know as little as ourselves (even if they are much followed ancient or modern philosophers).

Contemplation. This is careful and logical thought which directs observation and draws conclusions. It is not merely open-ended thought but has the divine purposes of science in mind. (Proverbs 6:6)

Description. This is being able to communicate, in clear unambiguous (as much as is possible) and sequenced language (and drawing), observations and conclusions. (1 Kings 4:38)

It includes knowing the difference between correlation and cause and effect. This needs to be as honest as possible. Science is about discovering and communicating truth.

Listening. Having the humility and ability to draw on the accumulated wisdom of the past. This requires attentiveness and discernment. We have the responsibility to examine the lives, the message and the discoveries of those who have gone before. (1 Kings 4:34)

What the Bible says about the purpose of science

Worship. To bring praise and glory to God. If we have the Creator in mind as we study, it will be inevitable that our study will evoke a response of immense respect, gratitude, wonder and awe toward God. (Psalm 19, Psalm 97:6, Psalm 148, Revelation 4:11) Therefore, science enhances our *worship.*

Work. To take dominion over the Earth. Our understanding of creation – the foundations and inter-relations of the particulars will enable us to develop means of managing (i.e. developing and conserving) the Earth. Modern technological advance is rooted in scientific understanding and, when guided by the principles and values of the Bible, advances human flourishing to the glory of God. (Genesis 1:28) Therefore, science enhances our *work.*

Wisdom. To help us understand God and His principles. As we learn about various aspects of creation and reflect on their significance and analogies of our relationship with God and others, we gain insight from God. (Job 12:7-8, Proverbs 6:6-8, Matthew 6:26-34) Hence, science enhances our *wisdom.*

The end result of science properly done in relationship with God and faithfully applied is human flourishing. Thus, the outcomes in the areas of *worship, work and wisdom* should become the motivating attitudes directing and inspiring our study.

What might we then do?

Listen to the voice of God. God speaks in His Word, the Bible. God speaks in His works, His creation. He gives us our senses to listen. He gives us our reason to meditate. He gives us His Spirit to confirm what we hear. To aid our listening, He gives us those who have studied before us – Bible scholars or ministers to help us interpret what God is saying in His Word, the Bible and scientists and researchers to interpret creation.

Obey the voice of the Lord. We ignore the word of the Lord at our peril. If we disregard the law of gravity or the second law of thermodynamics (heat transfer), we will get hurt and burnt! If we disregard God's word to repent, to love, or to believe, we will suffer the consequences. However, if we obey God's word, in creation and the Bible, we will flourish and enjoy the blessings that God planned for us.

Use our resources to glorify God. If we use the knowledge and technology we now have at hand to love others and to cause others to flourish, we are outworking the kingdom of God, and glorifying Him.

Share the Word of the Lord. Share what you have learned from Him, so that others may hear, obey and be blessed. Always point to Jesus.

Worship Him. Creation in all its awesomeness demands our worship of the creator. He alone is worthy of praise. He is absolutely awesome. 'For from Him and through Him and for Him are all things. To Him be the glory for ever.' (Romans 11:36)

Discussion

What will I do as a result of this study? What can we do together now?

FURTHER READING

This short list of readings is just a few of many books or articles on the topic. The books listed are just a sample of the writings of these authors. I particularly recommend the writings of John Lennox and Vishal Mangalwadi and Dan Graves' book for an historical perspective. If you want to read more I suggest you do your own search for readings on the topic. They are numerous.

Needless to say, I am not suggesting I agree with everything these authors say. Indeed, I take a different stance on some significant issues with some, but I find their writing is helpful in stimulating my thinking on the topic and helps me get a better grasp of what the Bible says and of the amazing imagination, power, love and glory of God.

Graves, Dan, *Scientists of Faith: Forty-eight biographies of scientists and their Christian faith,* (1996)

Lennox, John C, *God's Undertaker: Has science buried God?* (2007)

Lennox, John C, *Seven Days that Divide the World: The beginning according to Genesis and science,* Zondervan (2011)

Mangalwadi, Vishal, *The Book that Made Your World: How the Bible created the soul of western civilization,* Thomas Nelson (2011)

Morris, Henry M, *Men of Science, Men of God* (1982)

Morris, Henry M, *The Biblical Basis for Modern Science* (1984)

Morris, Henry M, *Science and the Bible* (1986)

Pearcey, Nancy R, and Thaxton, Charles B, *The Soul of Science,* Crossway Books (1994)

Ross, Hugh, *Why the Universe is the Way it Is,* Baker Books (2008)

Ross, Hugh, *Navigating Genesis: A Scientist's Journey through Genesis 1-11* (2014)

Some examples of biographies of scientists for the non-academic reader:

Tiner, John Hudson, *Johannes Kepler: Giant of faith and science,* Mott Media (1977)

Tiner, John Hudson, *Robert Boyle: Trailblazer of science,* Mott Media (1989)

Tiner, John Hudson, *Isaac Newton: Inventor scientist and teacher,* Mott Media (1975)

Tiner, John Hudson, *Lois Pasteur, Founder of modern medicine,* Mott Media (1990)

Collins, David, *George Washington Carver: Man's slave becomes God's scientist,* Mott Media (1981)

Ludwig, Charles, *Michael Faraday, Father of Electronics,* Herald Press (1978)

Albus, Harry J, *The Peanut Man: The story of George Washington Carver*, Pickering and Inglis

THANKS

Thanks to those whose encouragement and practical help enabled this book to be produced – Andrew, Andrew, Bev, Chelsea, Craig, Francine, Gavin, Joanne, Rodney, Ruth and others.

www.ingramcontent.com/pod-product-compliance
Ingram Content Group UK Ltd.
Pitfield, Milton Keynes, MK11 3LW, UK
UKHW020240250726
13967UKWH00001B/476